Table of Contents

Folded Paper Puppets

Paper Bag Puppets

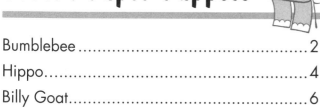

Paper Mitt Puppets

ABC Finger Puppets

Bumblebee
Folded Paper Puppet

Materials

- 9" x 18" (23 x 45.5 cm) yellow construction paper
- patterns on page 3
- marking pens or crayons
- scissors
- glue

Steps to Follow

1. Make the basic folded puppet out of the construction paper.

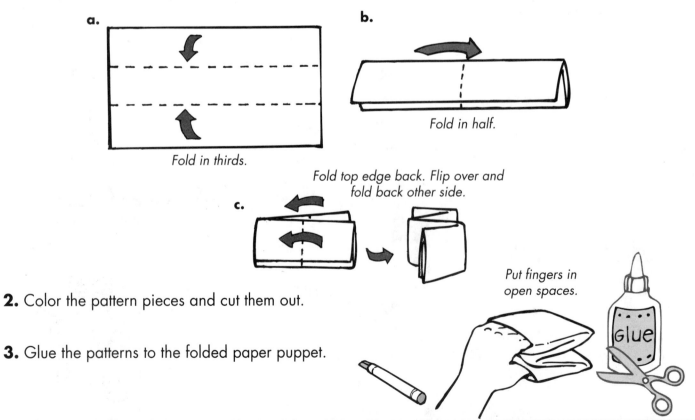

a.

Fold in thirds.

b.

Fold in half.

Fold top edge back. Flip over and fold back other side.

c.

Put fingers in open spaces.

2. Color the pattern pieces and cut them out.

3. Glue the patterns to the folded paper puppet.

Glue

Folded Paper Puppet Patterns

Bumblebee

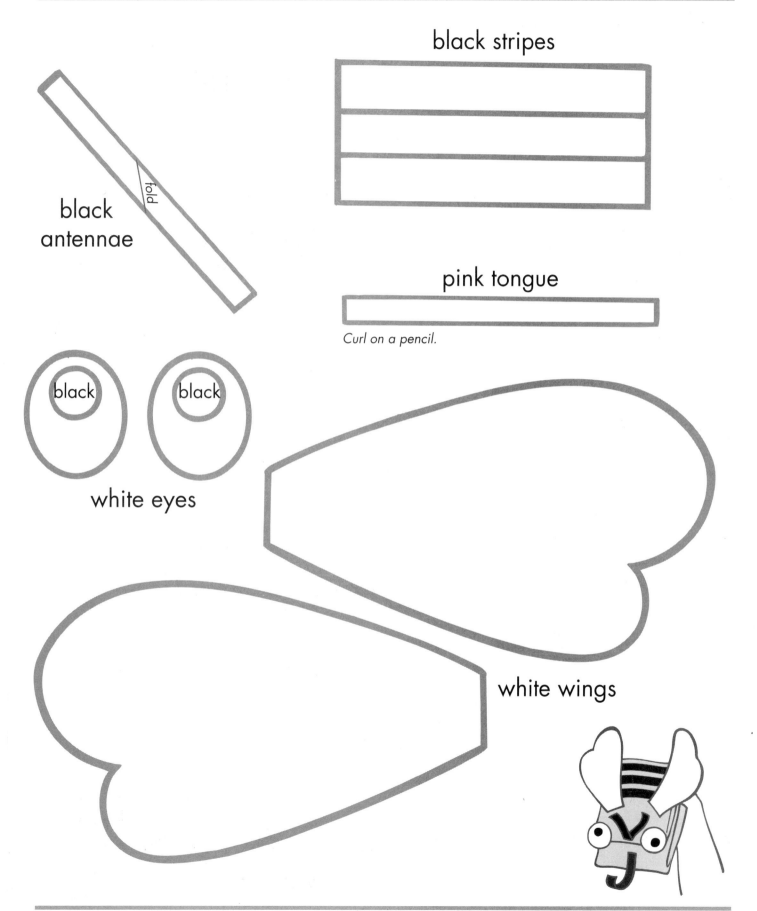

black stripes

black antennae

fold

pink tongue

Curl on a pencil.

black

black

white eyes

white wings

Hippo
Folded Paper Puppet

Materials

- 9" x 18" (23 x 45.5 cm) gray construction paper
- patterns on page 5
- marking pens or crayons
- scissors
- glue

Steps to Follow

1. Make the basic folded puppet out of the construction paper.

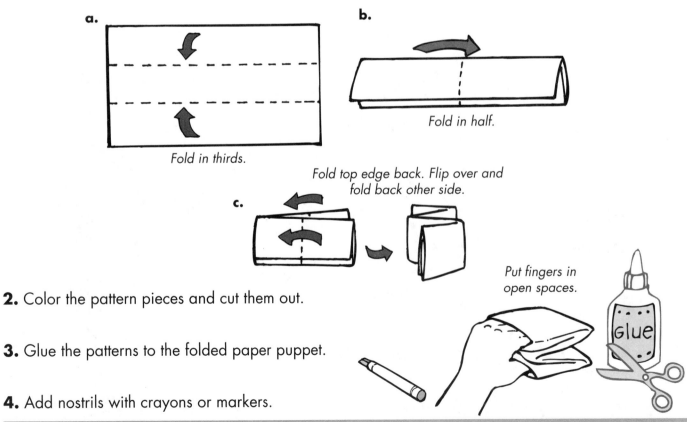

a.

Fold in thirds.

b.

Fold in half.

Fold top edge back. Flip over and fold back other side.

c.

Put fingers in open spaces.

2. Color the pattern pieces and cut them out.

3. Glue the patterns to the folded paper puppet.

4. Add nostrils with crayons or markers.

gray ears with
pink centers

fold

fold

gray legs with pink toes

fold

fold

white teeth

fold   fold

eyes

pink
tongue

5

Billy Goat
Folded Paper Puppet

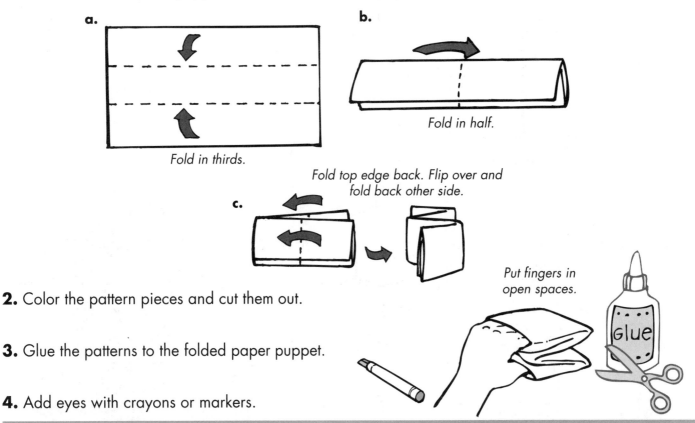

Materials

- 9" x 18" (23 x 45.5 cm) white construction paper
- patterns on page 7
- marking pens or crayons
- scissors
- glue

Steps to Follow

1. Make the basic folded puppet out of the construction paper.

a.

Fold in thirds.

b.

Fold in half.

c.

Fold top edge back. Flip over and fold back other side.

Put fingers in open spaces.

Glue

2. Color the pattern pieces and cut them out.

3. Glue the patterns to the folded paper puppet.

4. Add eyes with crayons or markers.

Folded Paper Puppet Patterns

Billy Goat

white beard

fold

gray ears

brown horns

pink tongue

fold

Curl horns over a pencil.

white snout

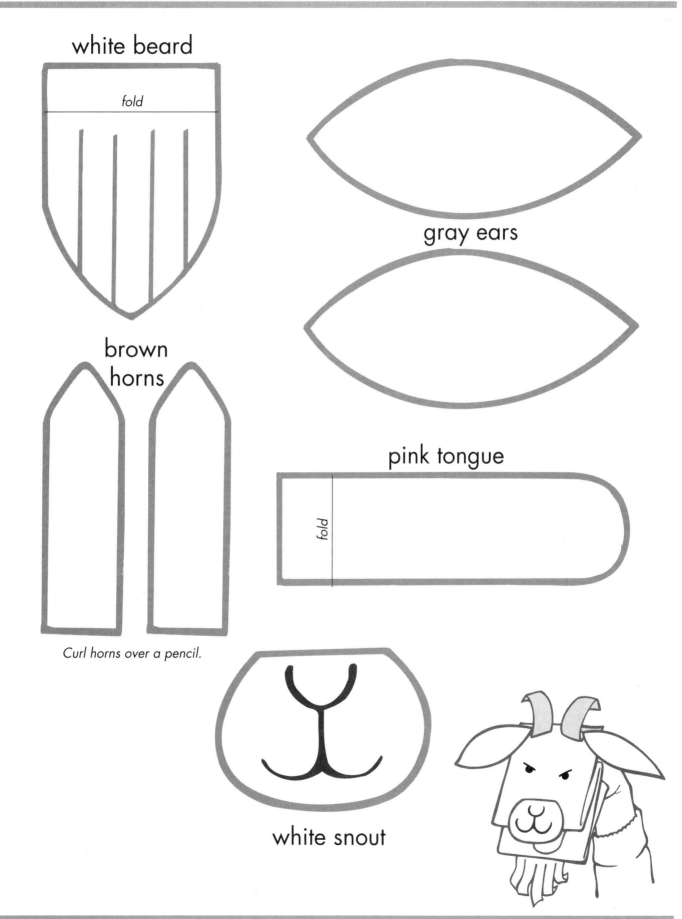

Jackrabbit

Folded Paper Puppet

Materials

- 9" x 18" (23 x 45.5 cm) brown construction paper
- patterns on page 9
- marking pens or crayons
- scissors
- glue

Steps to Follow

1. Make the basic folded puppet out of the construction paper.

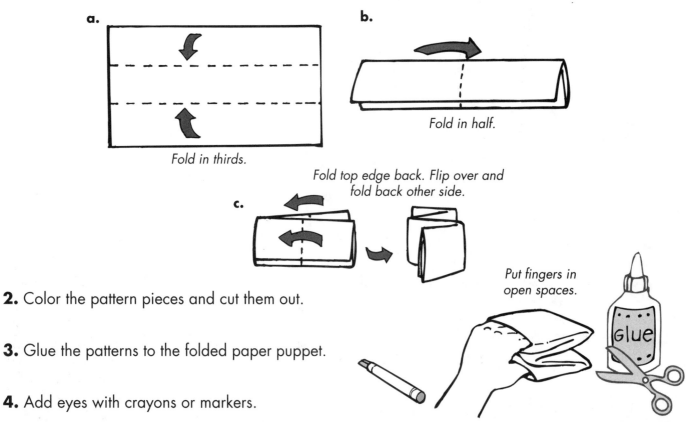

a.

Fold in thirds.

b.

Fold in half.

Fold top edge back. Flip over and fold back other side.

c.

Put fingers in open spaces.

2. Color the pattern pieces and cut them out.

3. Glue the patterns to the folded paper puppet.

4. Add eyes with crayons or markers.

Folded Paper Puppet Patterns

Jackrabbit

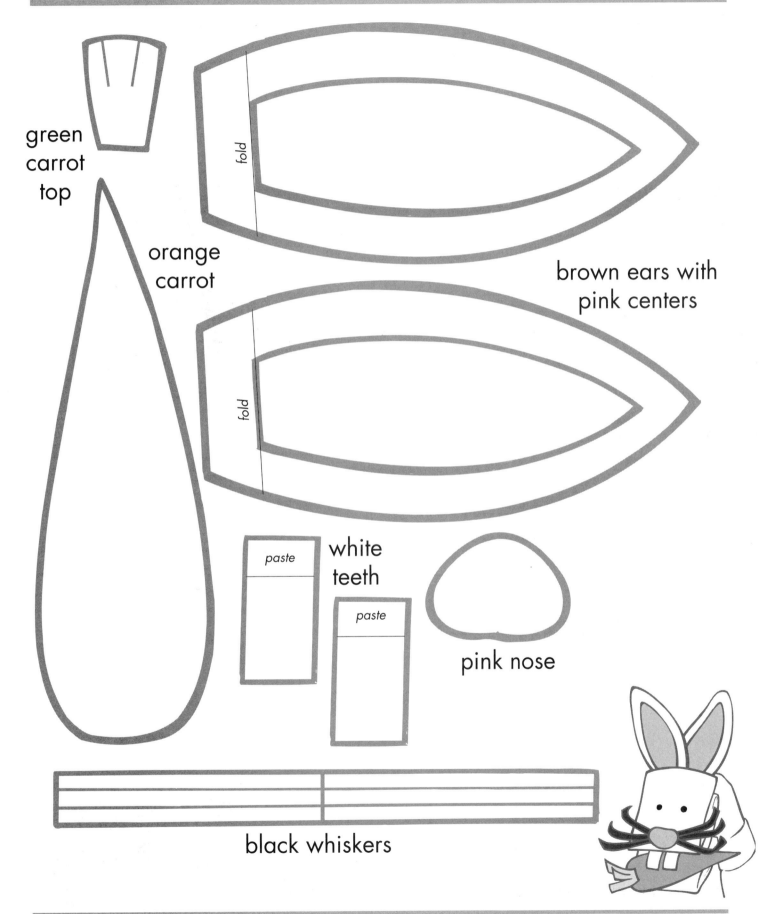

green carrot top

orange carrot

brown ears with pink centers

fold

fold

paste

paste

white teeth

pink nose

black whiskers

Frog
Folded Paper Puppet

Materials

- 9" x 18" (23 x 45.5 cm) green construction paper
- patterns on page 11
- marking pens or crayons
- scissors
- glue

Steps to Follow

1. Make the basic folded puppet out of the construction paper.

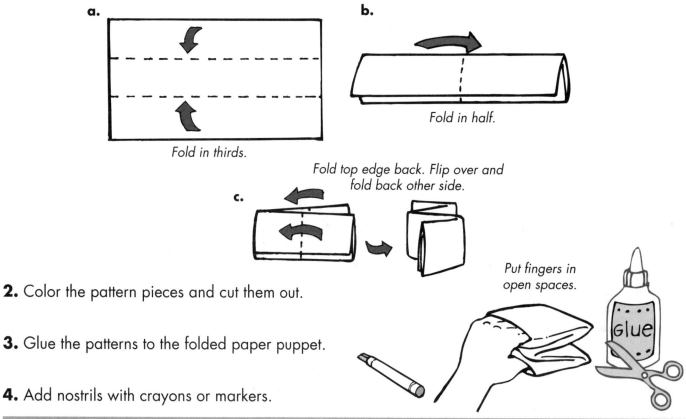

a.

Fold in thirds.

b.

Fold in half.

Fold top edge back. Flip over and fold back other side.

c.

Put fingers in open spaces.

2. Color the pattern pieces and cut them out.

3. Glue the patterns to the folded paper puppet.

4. Add nostrils with crayons or markers.

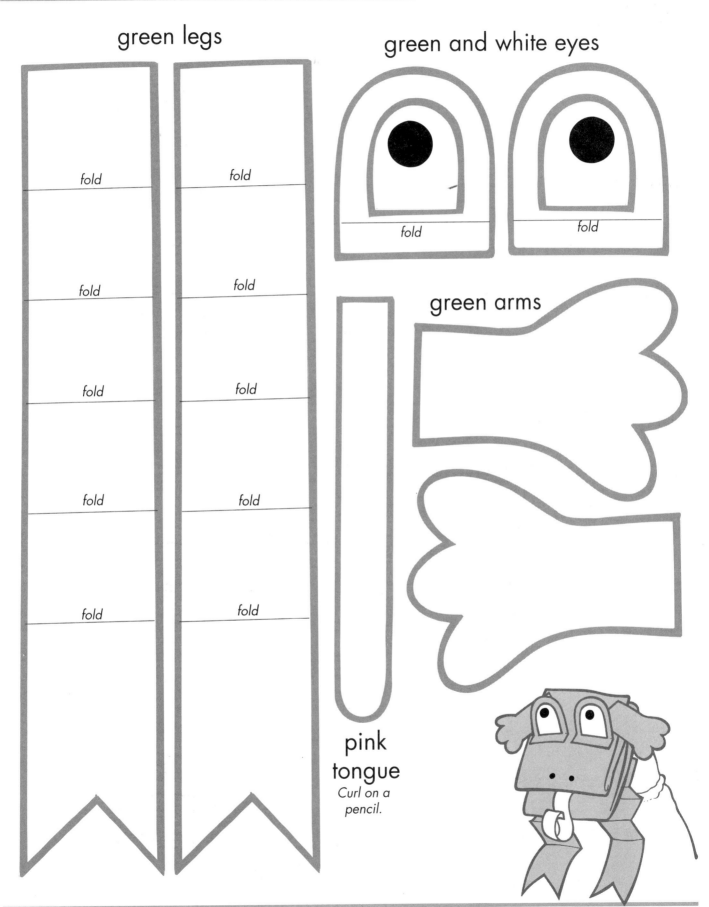

green legs

green and white eyes

fold

fold

fold

fold

fold

fold

fold

fold

green arms

fold

fold

fold

fold

fold

fold

pink
tongue
*Curl on a
pencil.*

Bluebird
Folded Paper Puppet

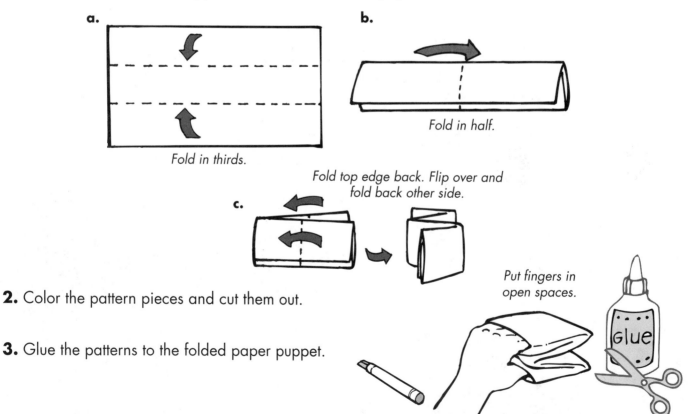

Materials

- 9" x 18" (23 x 45.5 cm) blue construction paper
- patterns on page 13
- marking pens or crayons
- scissors
- glue

Steps to Follow

1. Make the basic folded puppet out of the construction paper.

a.

Fold in thirds.

b.

Fold in half.

Fold top edge back. Flip over and fold back other side.

c.

Put fingers in open spaces.

2. Color the pattern pieces and cut them out.

3. Glue the patterns to the folded paper puppet.

glue

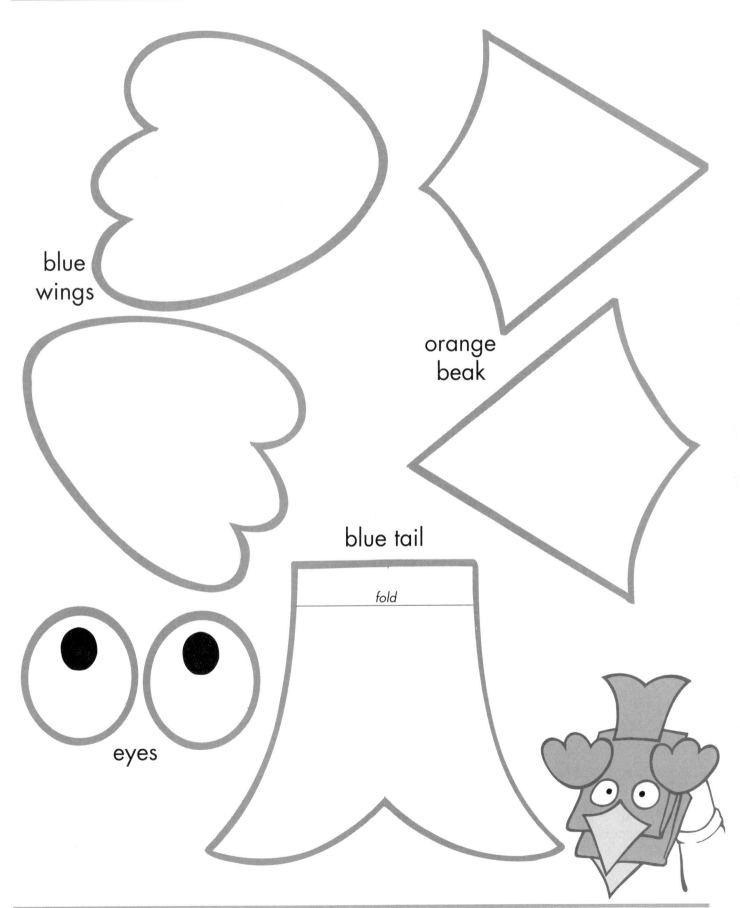

blue
wings

orange
beak

blue tail

fold

eyes

Dragon
Folded Paper Puppet

Materials

- 9" x 18" (23 x 45.5 cm) green construction paper
- patterns on page 15
- marking pens or crayons
- scissors
- glue

Steps to Follow

1. Make the basic folded puppet out of the construction paper.

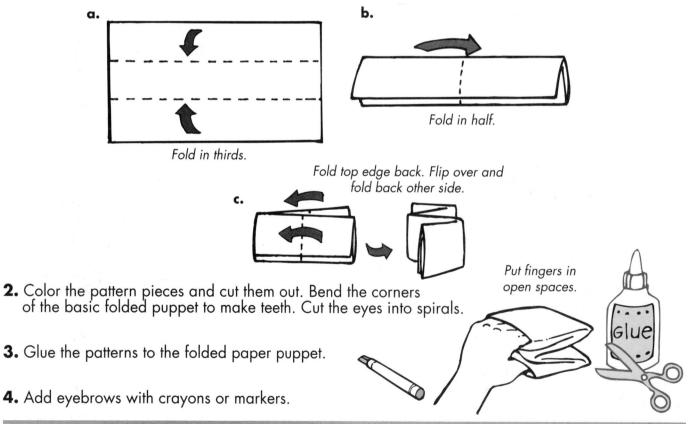

a.

Fold in thirds.

b.

Fold in half.

c.

Fold top edge back. Flip over and fold back other side.

Put fingers in open spaces.

2. Color the pattern pieces and cut them out. Bend the corners of the basic folded puppet to make teeth. Cut the eyes into spirals.

3. Glue the patterns to the folded paper puppet.

4. Add eyebrows with crayons or markers.

Folded Paper Puppet Patterns

Dragon

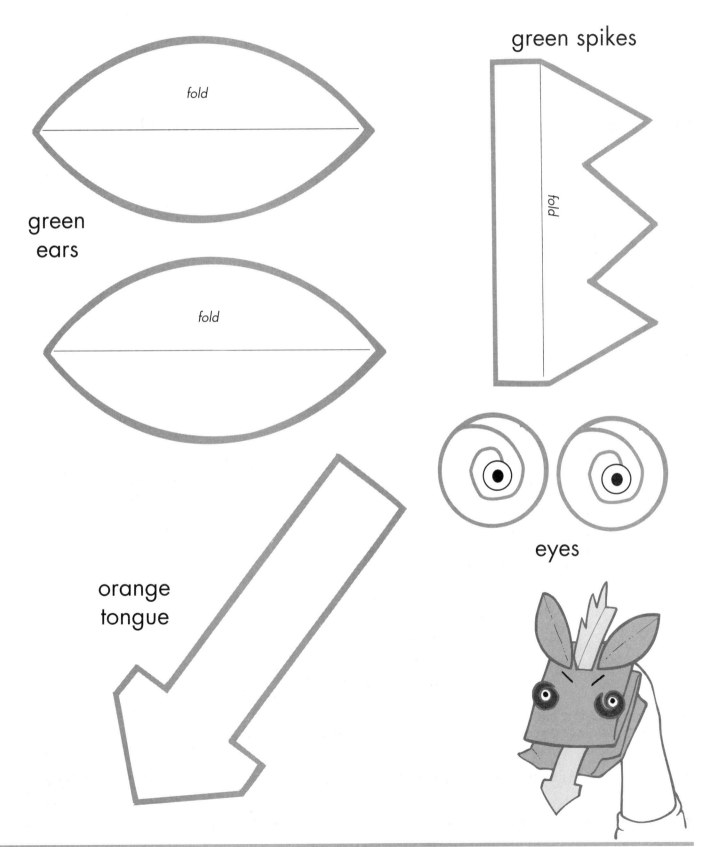

green spikes

fold

green
ears

fold

fold

eyes

orange
tongue

Cow

Folded Paper Puppet

Materials

- 9" x 18" (23 x 45.5 cm) brown construction paper
- patterns on page 17
- marking pens or crayons
- scissors
- glue

Steps to Follow

1. Make the basic folded puppet out of the construction paper.

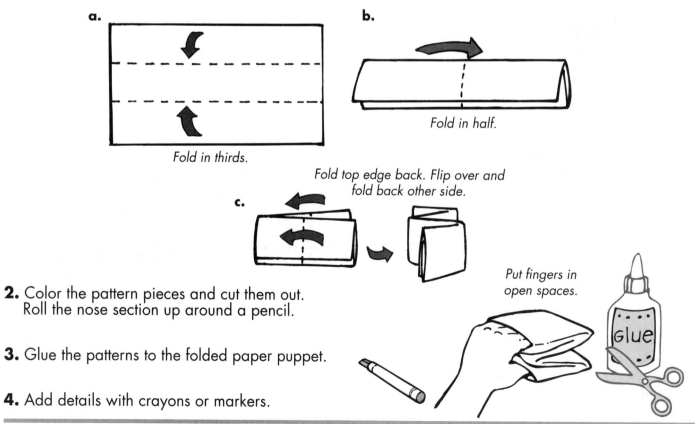

a.

Fold in thirds.

b.

Fold in half.

Fold top edge back. Flip over and fold back other side.

c.

Put fingers in open spaces.

Glue

2. Color the pattern pieces and cut them out. Roll the nose section up around a pencil.

3. Glue the patterns to the folded paper puppet.

4. Add details with crayons or markers.

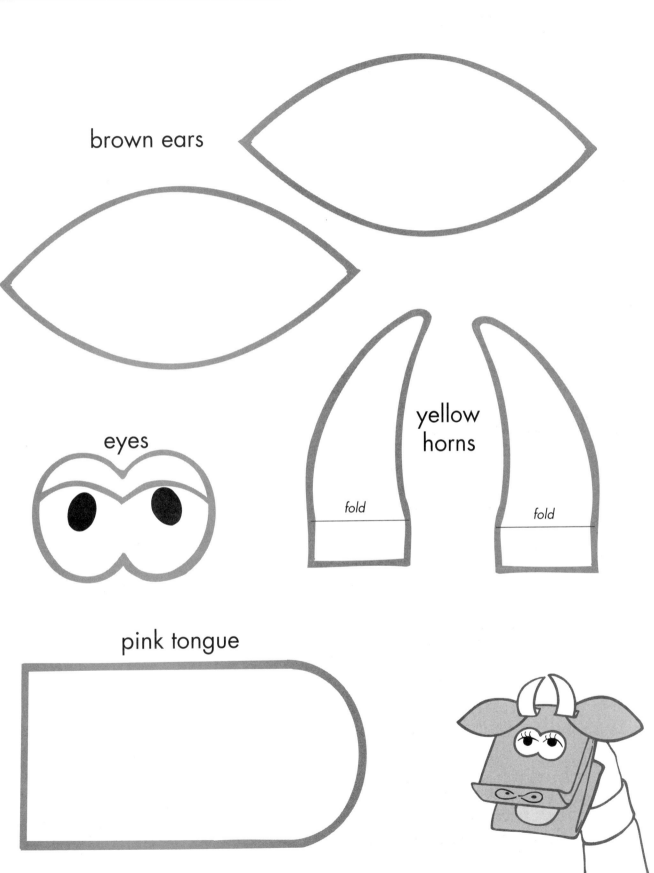

brown ears

eyes

yellow horns

fold   *fold*

pink tongue

Girl
Paper Bag Puppet

Materials

- a lunch-size paper bag
- patterns on the bottom of this page and page 19
- marking pens or crayons
- scissors
- glue

Steps to Follow

1. Color and cut out the patterns.
2. Glue the patterns to the paper bag.

Head pattern glued to the flap of the paper bag.

Body pattern glued to the bag.

head pattern

Paper Bag Puppet Patterns

body pattern

Boy
Paper Bag Puppet

Materials

- a lunch-size paper bag
- patterns on the bottom of this page and page 21
- marking pens or crayons
- scissors
- glue

Steps to Follow

1. Color and cut out the patterns.
2. Glue the patterns to the paper bag.

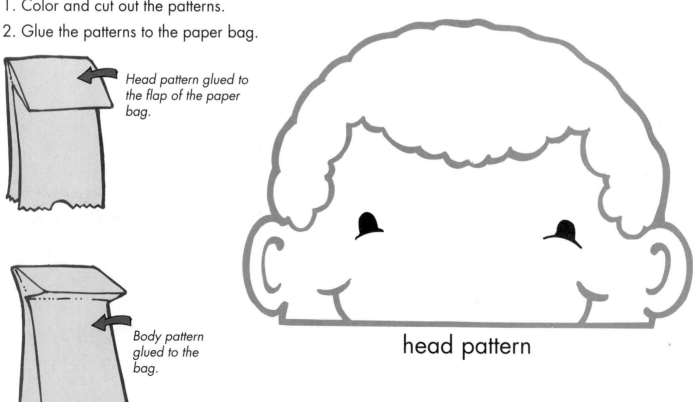

Head pattern glued to the flap of the paper bag.

Body pattern glued to the bag.

head pattern

body pattern

Alligator
Paper Bag Puppet

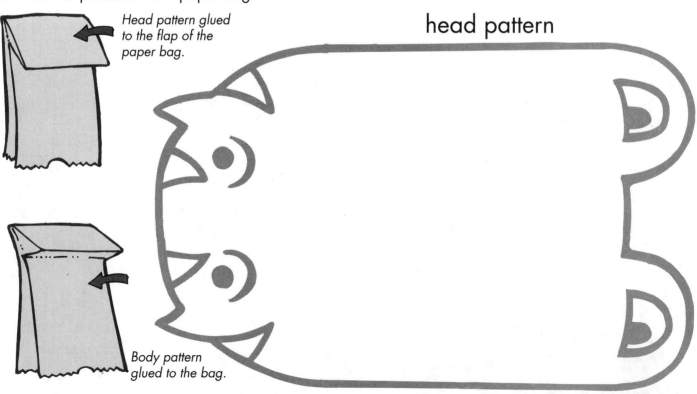

Materials

- a lunch-size paper bag
- patterns on the bottom of this page and page 23
- marking pens or crayons
- scissors
- glue

Steps to Follow

1. Color and cut out the patterns.
2. Glue the patterns to the paper bag.

Head pattern glued to the flap of the paper bag.

Body pattern glued to the bag.

head pattern

body pattern

Bat

Paper Bag Puppet

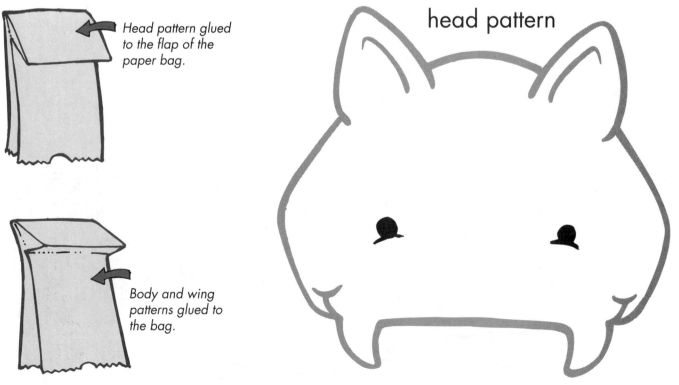

Materials

- a lunch-size paper bag
- patterns on the bottom of this page, page 25, and the inside back cover
- marking pens or crayons
- scissors
- glue

Steps to Follow

1. Color and cut out the patterns.
2. Glue the patterns to the paper bag.

Head pattern glued to the flap of the paper bag.

Body and wing patterns glued to the bag.

head pattern

body pattern

Duck

Paper Bag Puppet

Materials

- a lunch-size paper bag
- patterns on the bottom of this page and page 27
- marking pens or crayons
- scissors
- glue

Steps to Follow

1. Color and cut out the patterns.
2. Glue the patterns to the paper bag.

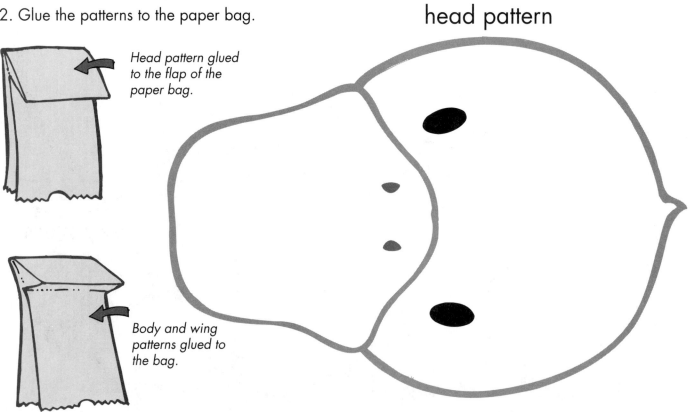

Head pattern glued to the flap of the paper bag.

Body and wing patterns glued to the bag.

head pattern

Paper Bag Puppet Patterns

Duck

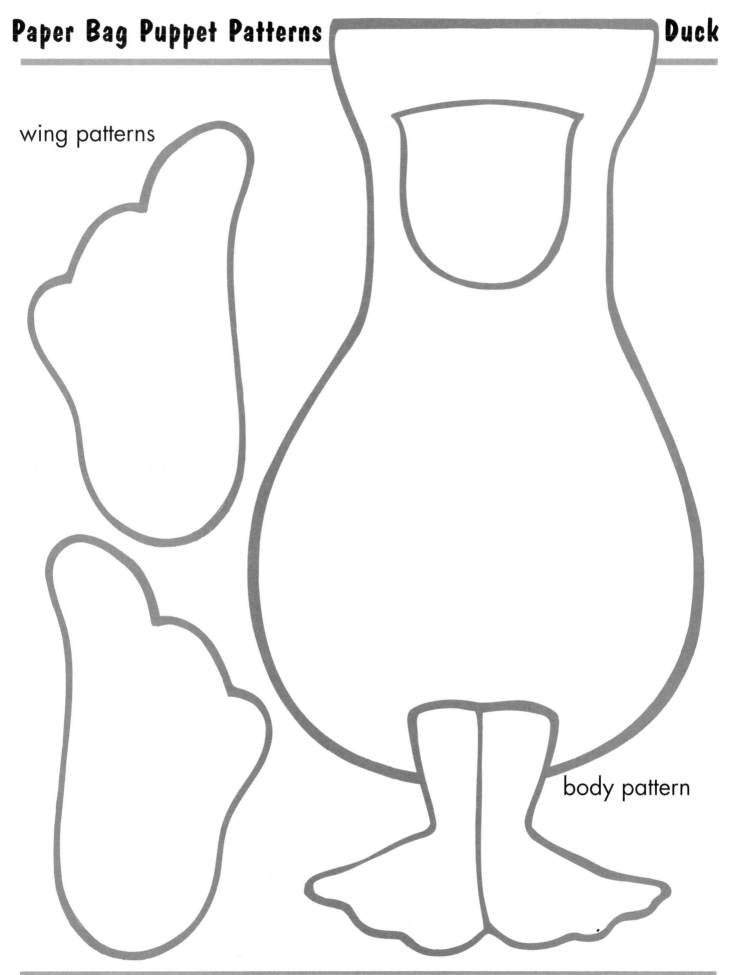

wing patterns

body pattern

How to Make Puppets with Children • EMC 762

Giraffe
Paper Bag Puppet

Materials

- a lunch-size paper bag
- patterns on the bottom of this page and page 29
- marking pens or crayons
- scissors
- glue

Steps to Follow

1. Color and cut out the patterns.
2. Glue the patterns to the paper bag.

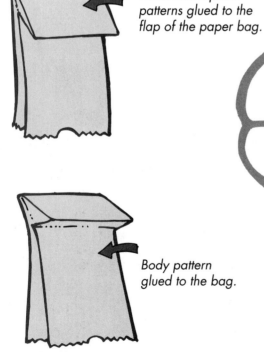

Head and topknot patterns glued to the flap of the paper bag.

Body pattern glued to the bag.

glue

head pattern

Paper Bag Puppet Patterns

Giraffe

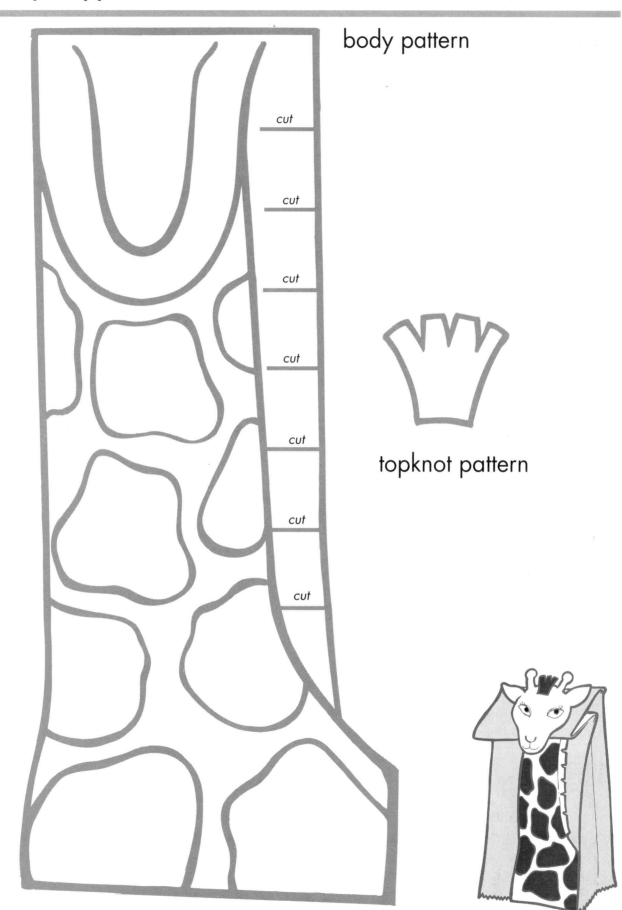

body pattern

cut

cut

cut

cut

cut

cut

cut

topknot pattern

Koala

Paper Bag Puppet

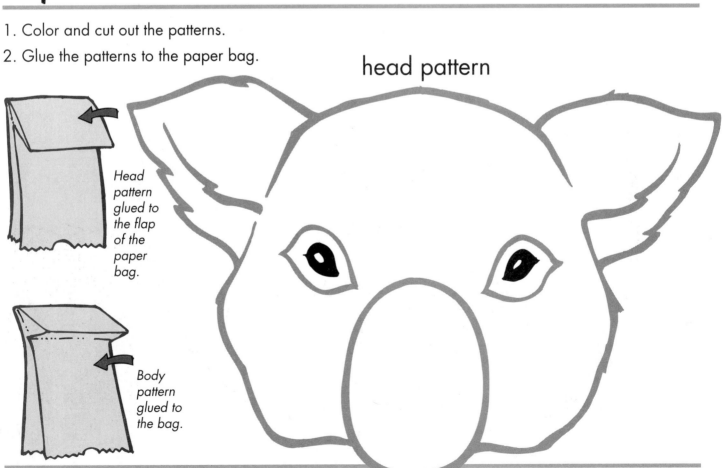

Materials

- a lunch-size paper bag
- patterns on the bottom this page and page 31
- marking pens or crayons
- scissors
- glue

Steps to Follow

1. Color and cut out the patterns.
2. Glue the patterns to the paper bag.

Head pattern glued to the flap of the paper bag.

Body pattern glued to the bag.

head pattern

body pattern

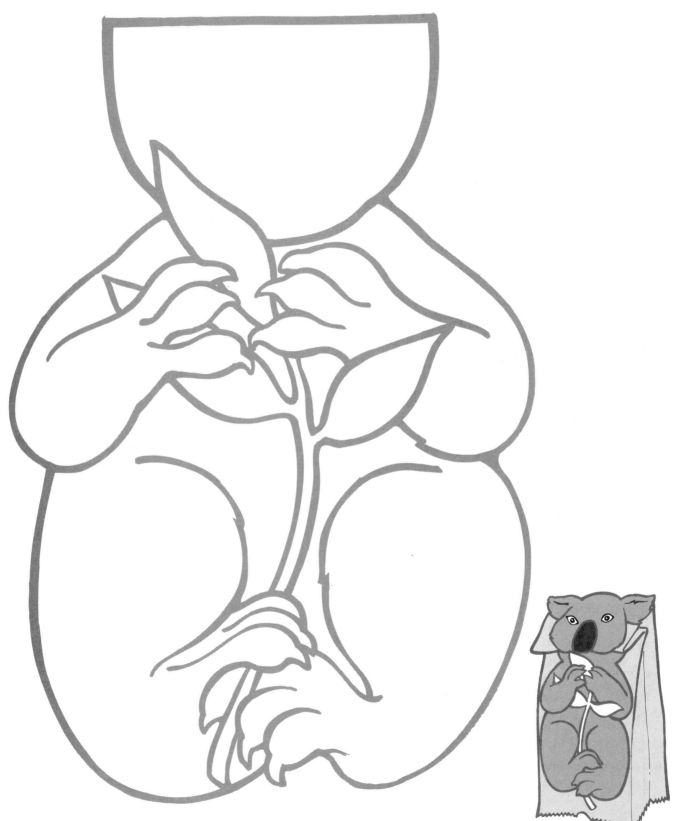

Bear

Paper Mitt Puppet

Materials

- 9" x 12" (23 x 30.5 cm) brown construction paper
- patterns on page 33
- marking pens or crayons
- scissors
- glue

Steps to Follow

1. Use the construction paper to make the basic mitt puppet.

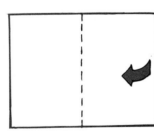

Fold in half.

Round the top.

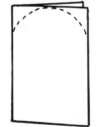

Open the paper and apply glue as shown.

Refold the paper and press firmly.

2. Color and cut out the pattern pieces.

3. Glue the patterns on the mitt.

4. Add freckles on the snout with crayons or marking pens.

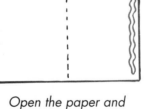

orange snout with black nose

eyes

brown ears with
orange centers

Raccoon
Paper Mitt Puppet

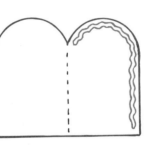

Materials

- 9" x 12" (23 x 30.5 cm) gray construction paper
- patterns on page 35
- marking pens or crayons
- scissors
- glue

Steps to Follow

1. Use the construction paper to make the basic mitt puppet.

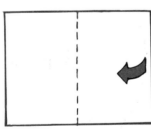

Fold in half.   *Round the top.*   *Open the paper and apply glue as shown.*   *Refold the paper and press firmly.*

2. Color and cut out the pattern pieces.

3. Glue the patterns on the mitt.

black mask and blue eyes

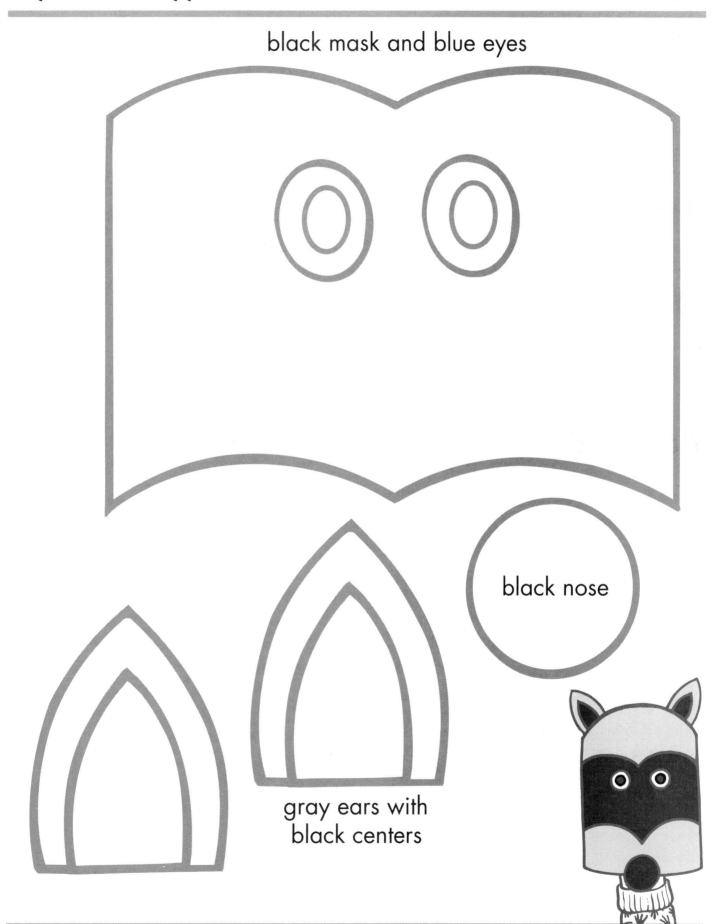

black nose

gray ears with
black centers

Hen

Paper Mitt Puppet

Materials

- 9" x 12" (23 x 30.5 cm) yellow construction paper
- patterns on page 37
- marking pens or crayons
- scissors
- glue

Steps to Follow

1. Use the construction paper to make the basic mitt puppet.

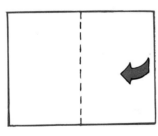

Fold in half.

Round the top.

Open the paper and apply glue as shown.

Refold the paper and press firmly.

2. Color and cut out the pattern pieces.

3. Glue the patterns on the mitt.

Paper Mitt Puppet Patterns

Hen

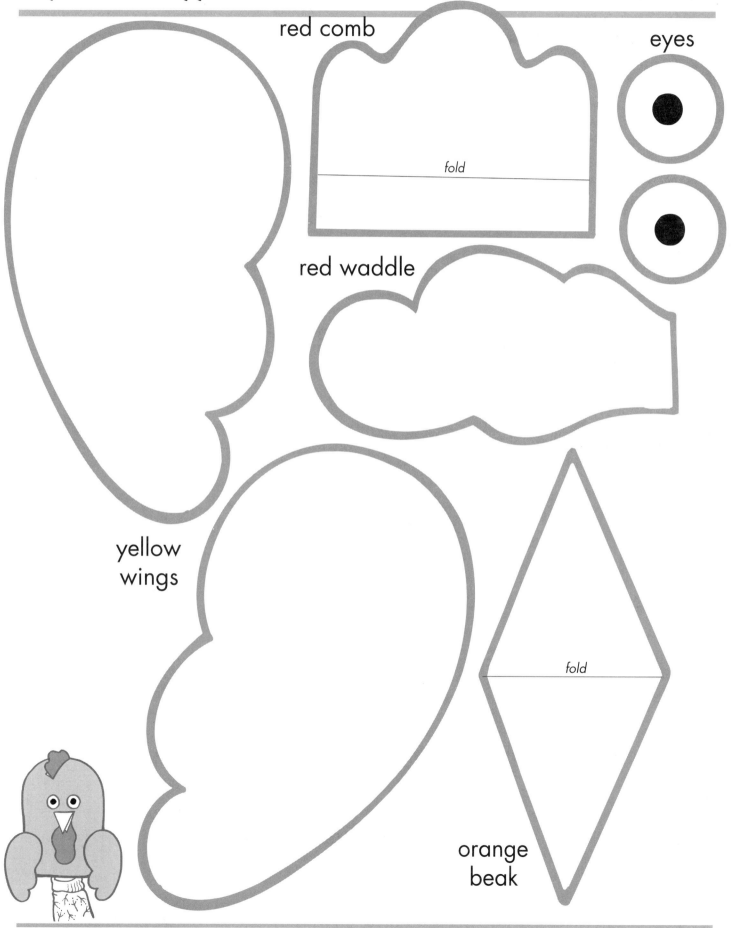

red comb

eyes

fold

red waddle

yellow
wings

orange
beak

fold

Walrus

Paper Mitt Puppet

Materials

- 9" x 12" (23 x 30.5 cm) brown construction paper
- patterns on page 39
- marking pens or crayons
- scissors
- glue

Steps to Follow

1. Use the construction paper to make the basic mitt puppet.

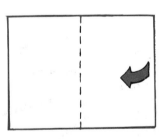

Fold in half.

Round the top.

Open the paper and apply glue as shown.

Refold the paper and press firmly.

2. Color and cut out the pattern pieces.

3. Glue the patterns on the mitt.

4. Add eyes with crayons or marking pens.

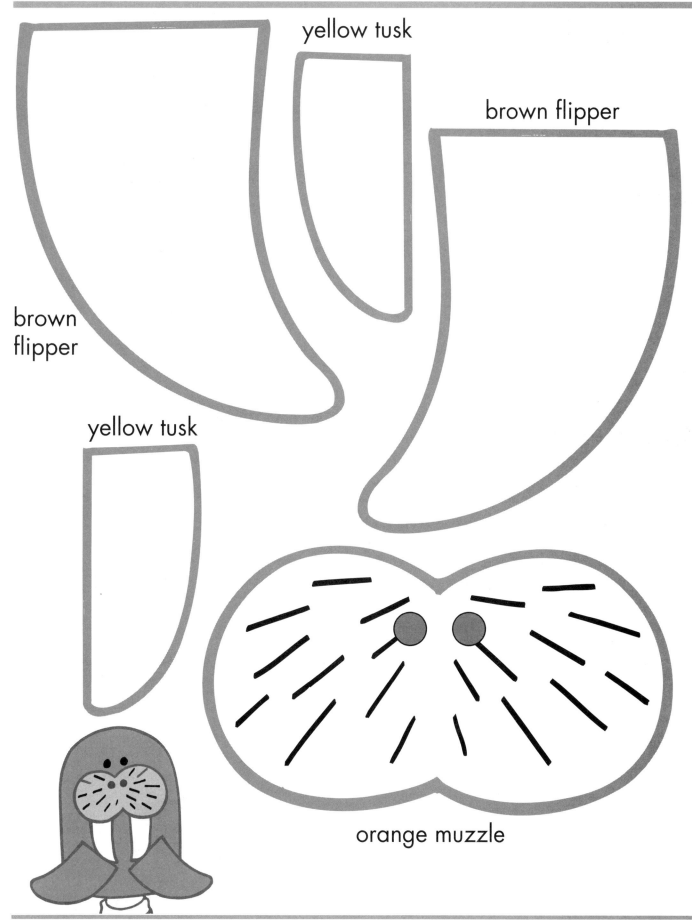

yellow tusk

brown flipper

brown flipper

yellow tusk

orange muzzle

Beaver

Paper Mitt Puppet

Materials

- 9" x 12" (23 x 30.5 cm) brown construction paper
- patterns on page 41
- marking pens or crayons
- scissors
- glue

Steps to Follow

1. Use the construction paper to make the basic mitt puppet.

Fold in half.

Round the top.

Open the paper and apply glue as shown.

Refold the paper and press firmly.

2. Color and cut out the pattern pieces.

3. Glue the patterns on the mitt.

4. Add eyes with crayons or marking pens.

Paper Mitt Puppet Patterns

Beaver

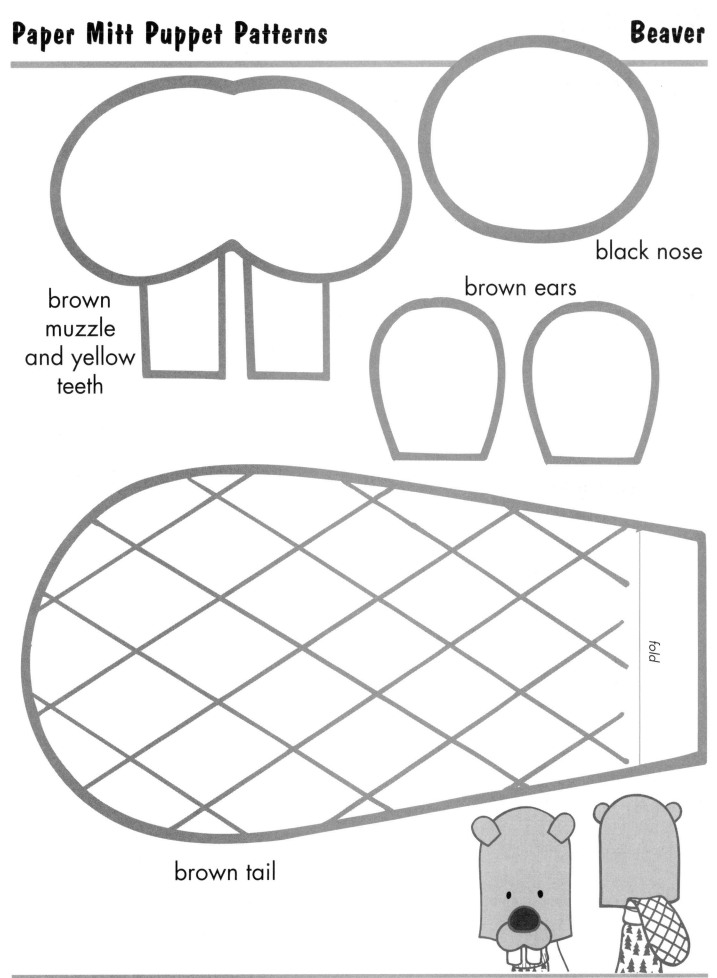

black nose

brown ears

brown
muzzle
and yellow
teeth

fold

brown tail

How to Make Puppets with Children • EMC 762

Monkey
Paper Mitt Puppet

Materials

- 9" x 12" (23 x 30.5 cm) brown construction paper
- patterns on page 43
- marking pens or crayons
- scissors
- glue

Steps to Follow

1. Use the construction paper to make the basic mitt puppet.

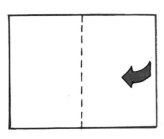

Fold in half.

Round the top.

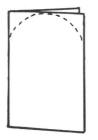

Open the paper and apply glue as shown.

Refold the paper and press firmly.

2. Color and cut out the pattern pieces.

3. Glue the patterns on the mitt.

orange face

brown
arms

brown
ears
with
orange
centers

Lamb

Paper Mitt Puppet

Materials

- 9" x 12" (23 x 30.5 cm) white construction paper
- patterns on page 45
- marking pens or crayons
- scissors
- glue

Steps to Follow

1. Use the construction paper to make the basic mitt puppet.

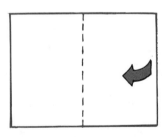
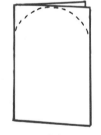
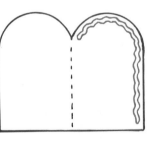

Fold in half.   *Round the top.*   *Open the paper and apply glue as shown.*   *Refold the paper and press firmly.*

2. Color and cut out the pattern pieces.

3. Glue the patterns on the mitt.

4. Add eyes with crayons or marking pens.

Paper Mitt Puppet Patterns

Lamb

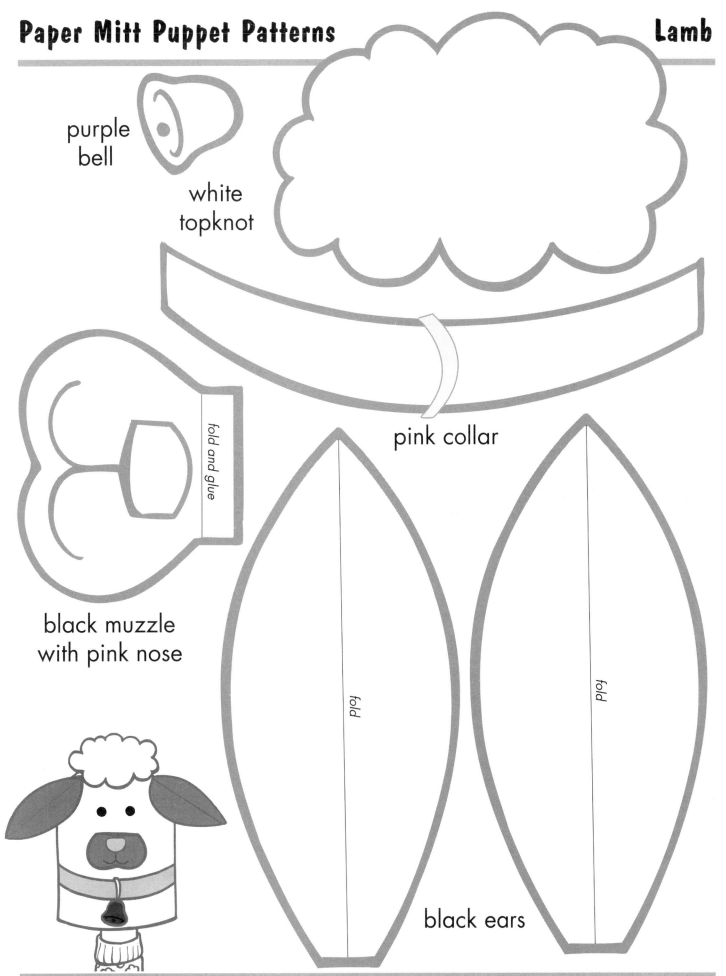

purple bell

white topknot

pink collar

fold and glue

black muzzle with pink nose

fold

fold

black ears

Cat

Paper Mitt Puppet

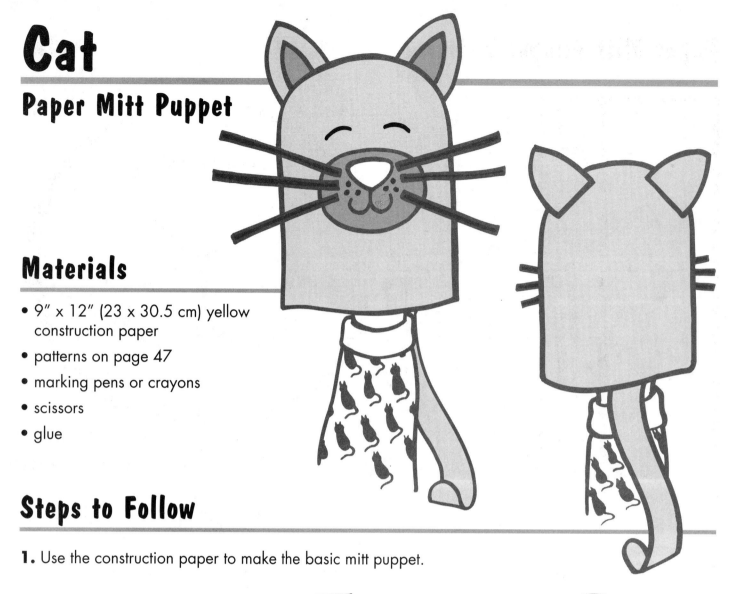

Materials

- 9" x 12" (23 x 30.5 cm) yellow construction paper
- patterns on page 47
- marking pens or crayons
- scissors
- glue

Steps to Follow

1. Use the construction paper to make the basic mitt puppet.

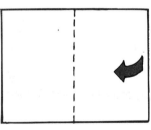 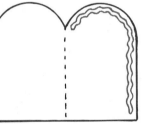 

Fold in half.   *Round the top.*   *Open the paper and apply glue as shown.*   *Refold the paper and press firmly.*

2. Color and cut out the pattern pieces.

3. Glue the patterns on the mitt.

4. Add eyes with crayons or marking pens.

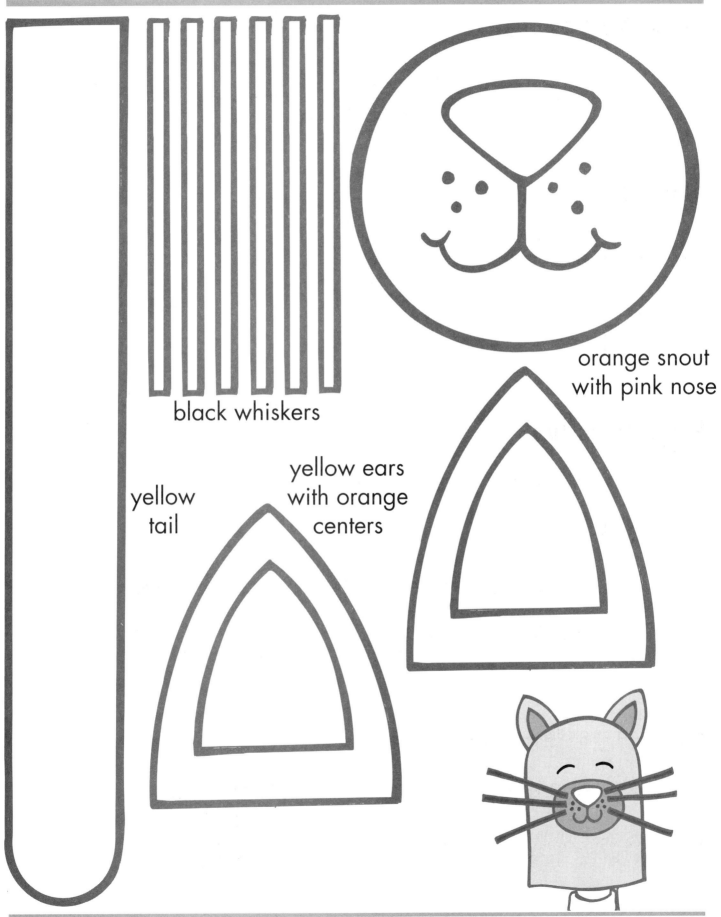

orange snout
with pink nose

black whiskers

yellow ears
with orange
centers

yellow
tail

Dog

Paper Mitt Puppet

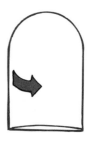

Materials

- 9" x 12" (23 x 30.5 cm) white construction paper
- patterns on page 49
- marking pens or crayons
- scissors
- glue

Steps to Follow

1. Use the construction paper to make the basic mitt puppet.

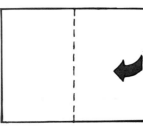

Fold in half.　　*Round the top.*　　*Open the paper and apply glue as shown.*　　*Refold the paper and press firmly.*

2. Color and cut out the pattern pieces.

3. Glue the patterns on the mitt.

4. Add freckles on the muzzle with crayons or marking pens.

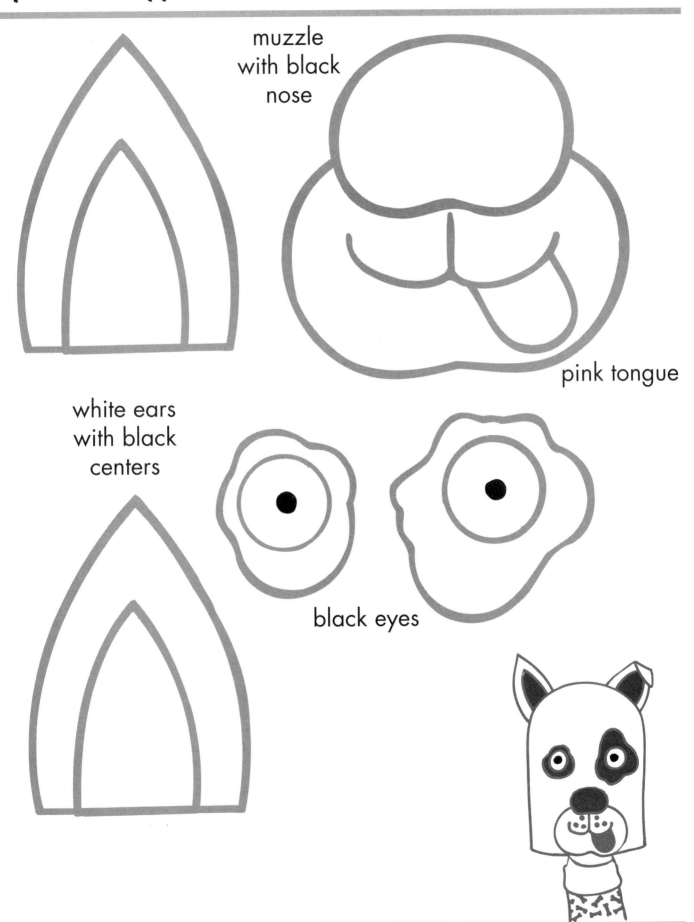

muzzle
with black
nose

pink tongue

white ears
with black
centers

black eyes

Mouse

Paper Mitt Puppet

Materials

- 9" x 12" (23 x 30.5 cm) gray construction paper
- patterns on page 51
- marking pens or crayons
- scissors
- glue

Steps to Follow

1. Use the construction paper to make the basic mitt puppet.

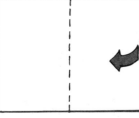

Fold in half. *Round the top.* *Open the paper and apply glue as shown.* *Refold the paper and press firmly.*

2. Color and cut out the pattern pieces.

3. Glue the patterns on the mitt.

4. Add eyes with crayons or marking pens.

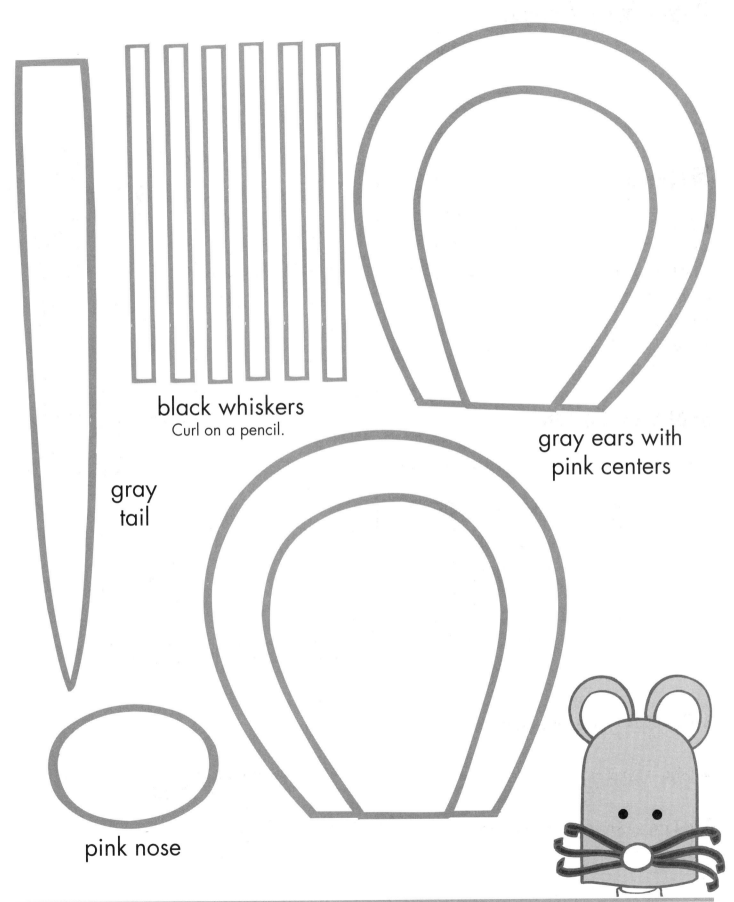

black whiskers
Curl on a pencil.

gray ears with
pink centers

gray
tail

pink nose

Pig
Paper Mitt Puppet

Materials

- 9" x 12" (23 x 30.5 cm) gray construction paper
- patterns on page 53
- marking pens or crayons
- scissors
- glue

Steps to Follow

1. Use the construction paper to make the basic mitt puppet.

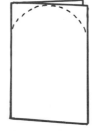

Fold in half.

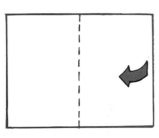

Round the top.

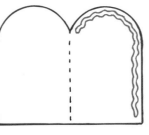

Open the paper and apply glue as shown.

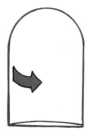

Refold the paper and press firmly.

2. Color and cut out the pattern pieces.

3. Glue the patterns on the mitt.

4. Add eyes with crayons or marking pens.

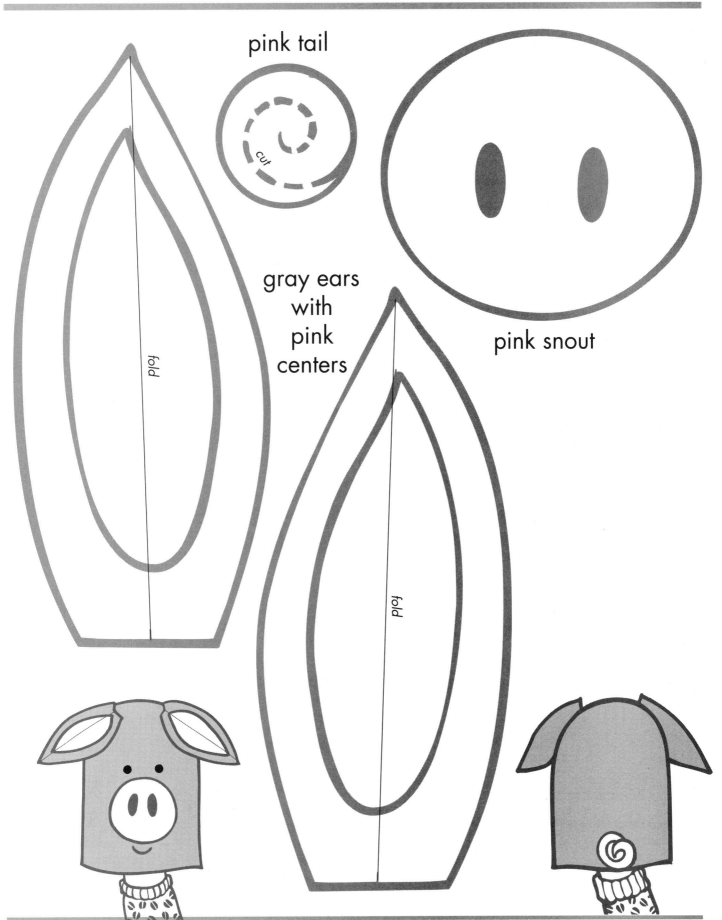

pink tail

gray ears
with
pink
centers

pink snout

fold

fold

cut

Snail

Paper Mitt Puppet

Materials

- 9" x 12" (23 x 30.5 cm) brown construction paper
- patterns on page 55
- piece of white roving–1 yard (0.9 m), cut in half
- marking pens or crayons
- scissors
- glue

Steps to Follow

1. Use the construction paper to make the basic mitt puppet.

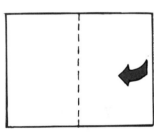

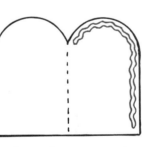

Fold in half.   *Round the top.*   *Open the paper and apply glue as shown.*   *Refold the paper and press firmly.*

2. Color and cut out the pattern pieces.

3. Glue the patterns on the mitt.

4. Make a spiral curl of glue on the mitt. Lay the white roving on the glue. Cut off any leftover roving. Repeat on the other side of the shell.

5. Add details with crayons or marking pens.

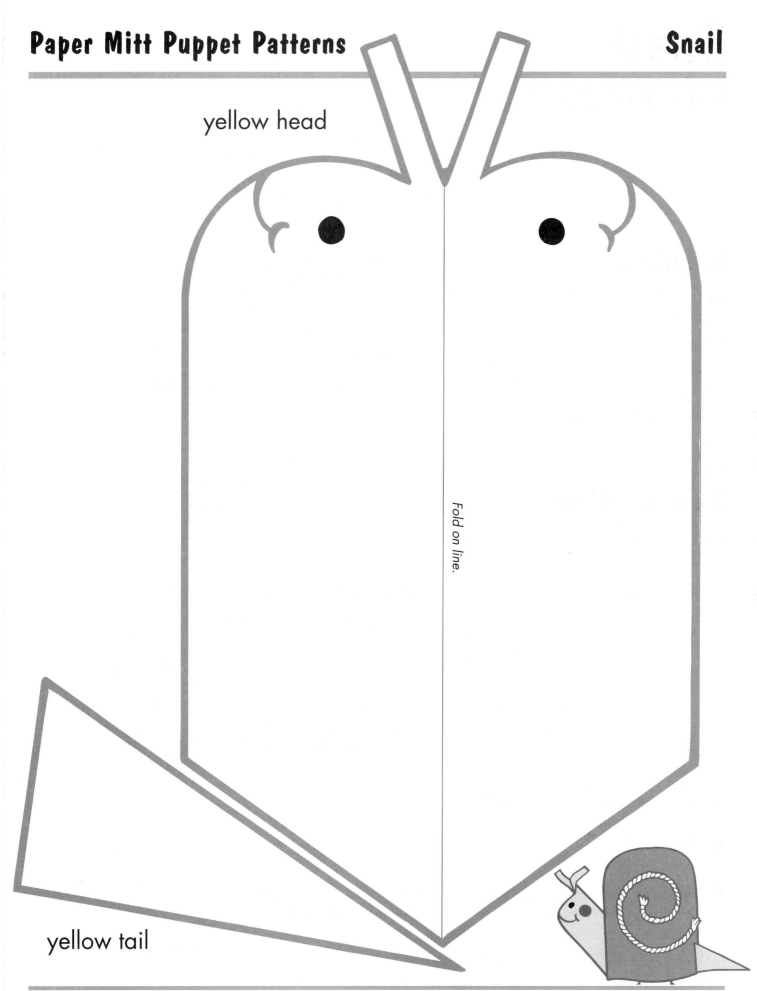

yellow head

Fold on line.

yellow tail

Lion

Paper Mitt Puppet

Materials

- 9" x 12" (23 x 30.5 cm) yellow construction paper
- patterns on page 57
- marking pens or crayons
- scissors
- glue

Steps to Follow

1. Use the construction paper to make the basic mitt puppet.

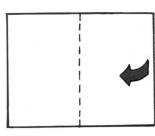 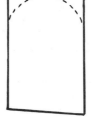

Fold in half.   *Round the top.*   *Open the paper and apply glue as shown.*   *Refold the paper and press firmly.*

2. Color and cut out the pattern pieces.

3. Glue the patterns on the mitt. Curl mane pieces over a pencil.

4. Add eyes and freckles on muzzle with crayons or marking pens.

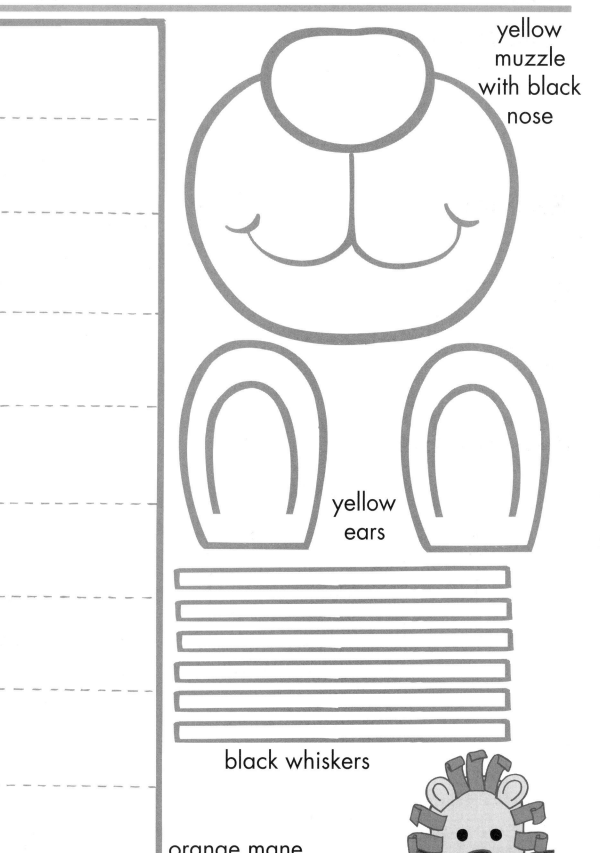

yellow
muzzle
with black
nose

yellow
ears

black whiskers

orange mane
Curl on a pencil.

Elephant

Paper Mitt Puppet

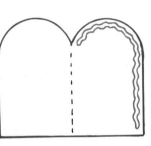

Materials

- 9" x 12" (23 x 30.5 cm) gray construction paper
- patterns on page 59
- marking pens or crayons
- scissors
- glue

Steps to Follow

1. Use the construction paper to make the basic mitt puppet.

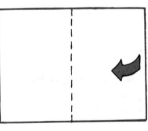

Fold in half.   *Round the top.*   *Open the paper and apply glue as shown.*   *Refold the paper and press firmly.*

2. Color and cut out the pattern pieces.

3. Glue the patterns on the mitt.

4. Add eyes with crayons or marking pens.

Paper Mitt Puppet Patterns

Elephant

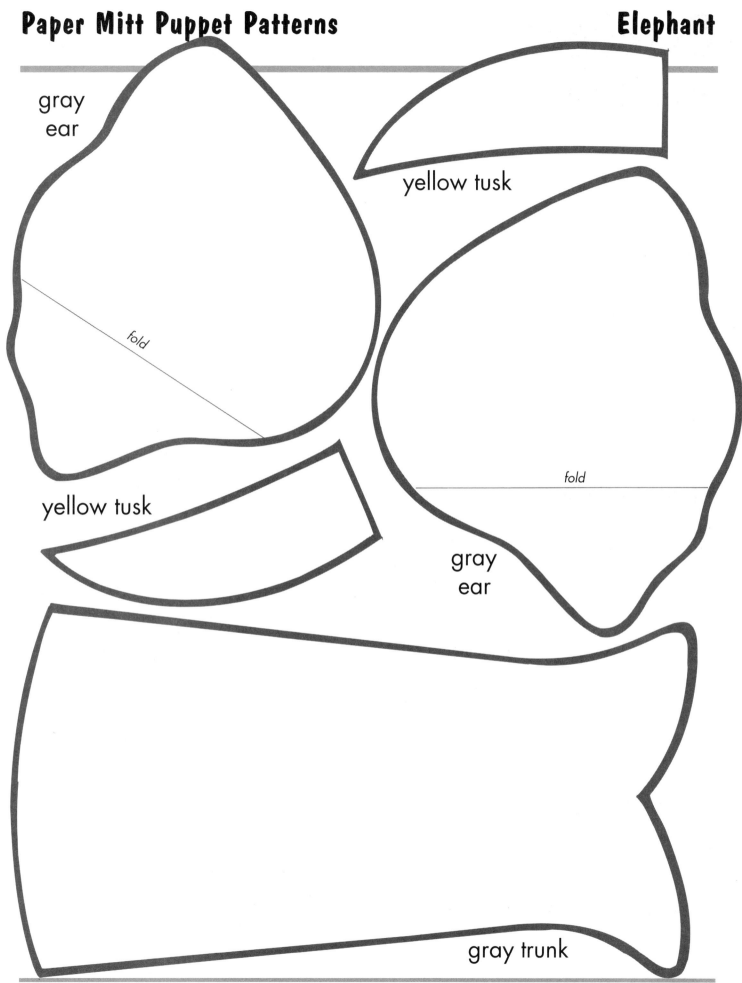

gray
ear

yellow tusk

fold

fold

yellow tusk

gray
ear

gray trunk

59

Octopus
Paper Mitt Puppet

Materials

- 9" x 12" (23 x 30.5 cm) light pink construction paper
- patterns on page 61
- marking pens or crayons
- scissors
- glue

Steps to Follow

1. Use the construction paper to make the basic mitt puppet.

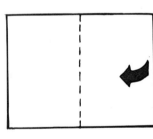

Fold in half.   *Round the top.*   *Open the paper and apply glue as shown.*   *Refold the paper and press firmly.*

2. Color and cut out the pattern pieces.

3. Glue the patterns on the mitt.

4. Add a mouth with crayons or marking pens.

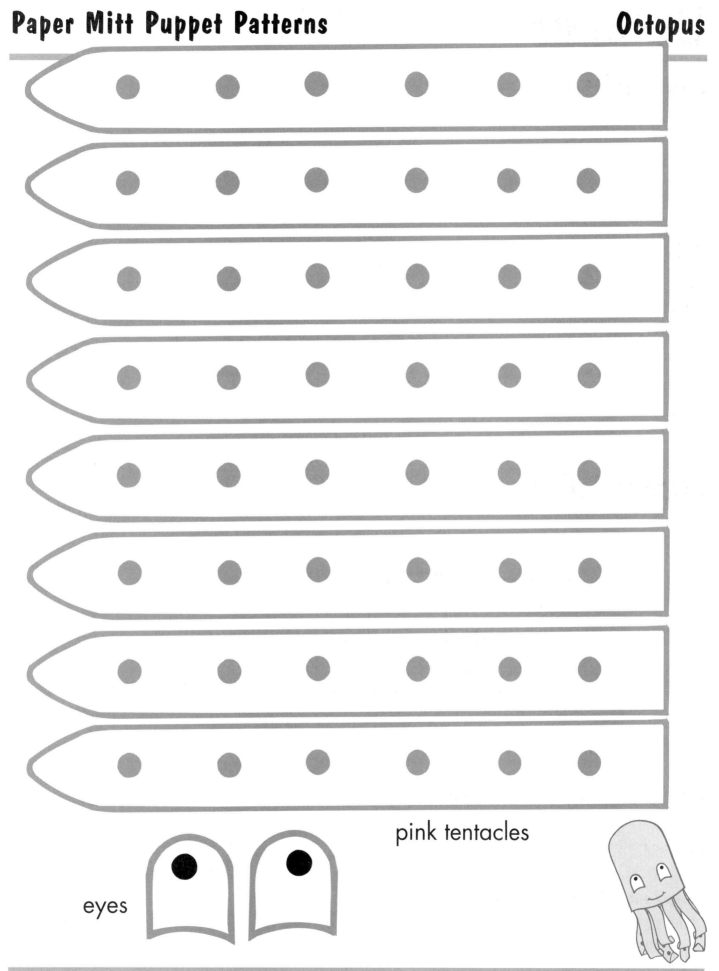

pink tentacles

eyes

Tortoise

Paper Mitt Puppet

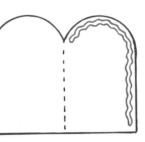

Materials

- 9" x 12" (23 x 30.5 cm) brown construction paper
- patterns on page 63
- marking pens or crayons
- scissors
- glue

Steps to Follow

1. Use the construction paper to make the basic mitt puppet.

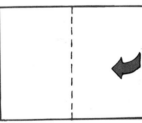

Fold in half. *Round the top.* *Open the paper and apply glue as shown.* *Refold the paper and press firmly.*

2. Color and cut out the pattern pieces.

3. Glue the patterns on the mitt.

4. Cut out the brown mitt between the front and back feet.

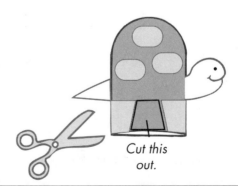

Cut this out.

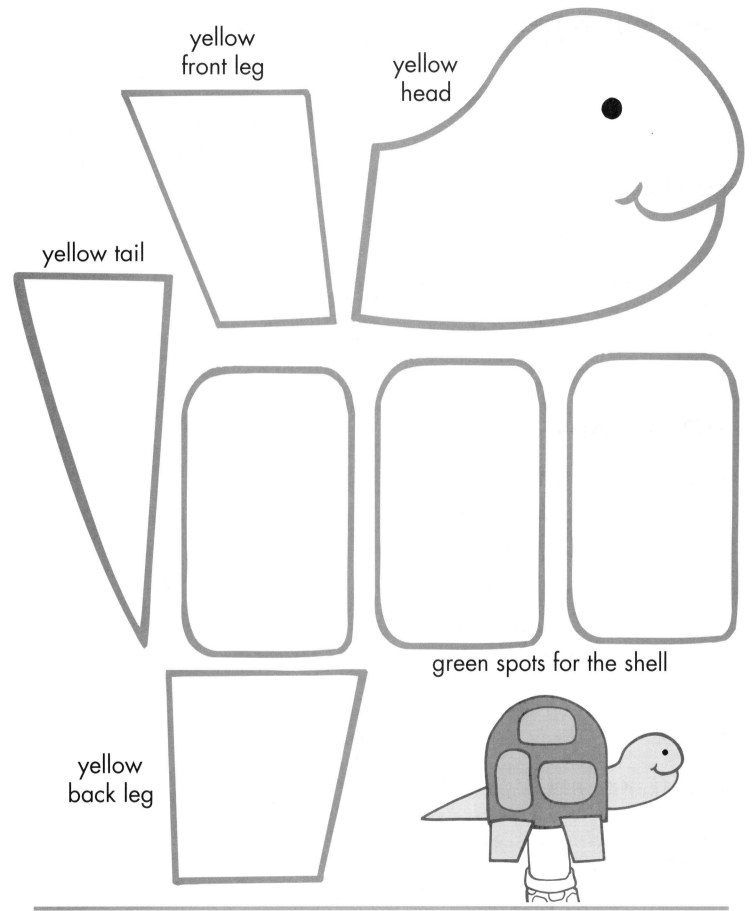

yellow
front leg

yellow
head

yellow tail

green spots for the shell

yellow
back leg

Whale

Paper Mitt Puppet

Materials

- 9" x 12" (23 x 30.5 cm) gray construction paper
- patterns on page 65
- marking pens or crayons
- scissors
- glue

Steps to Follow

1. Use the construction paper to make the basic mitt puppet.

Fold in half.

Round the top.

Open the paper and apply glue as shown.

Refold the paper and press firmly.

2. Color and cut out the pattern pieces.

3. Glue the patterns on the mitt.

4. Add a mouth with crayons or marking pens.

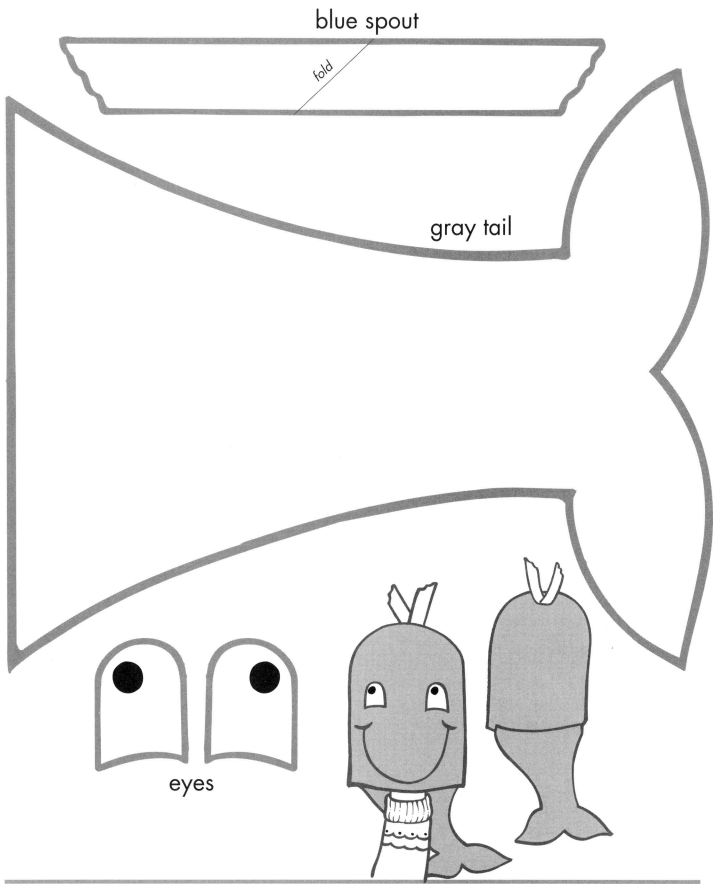

blue spout

fold

gray tail

eyes

Astronaut

Paper Mitt Puppet

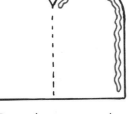

Materials

- 9" x 12" (23 x 30.5 cm) white construction paper
- patterns on page 67
- marking pens or crayons
- scissors
- glue

Steps to Follow

1. Use the construction paper to make the basic mitt puppet.

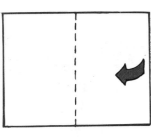
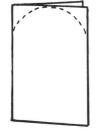

Fold in half.   *Round the top.*   *Open the paper and apply glue as shown.*   *Refold the paper and press firmly.*

2. Color the pattern pieces. (Students draw their own faces on the faceplate.) Cut out the patterns.

3. Glue the patterns on the mitt.

4. Add details with crayons or marking pens.

Paper Mitt Puppet Patterns

Astronaut

air
hose

fold

fold

fold

fold

fold

Draw your face here.

faceplate

oxygen

oxygen tank

earpieces

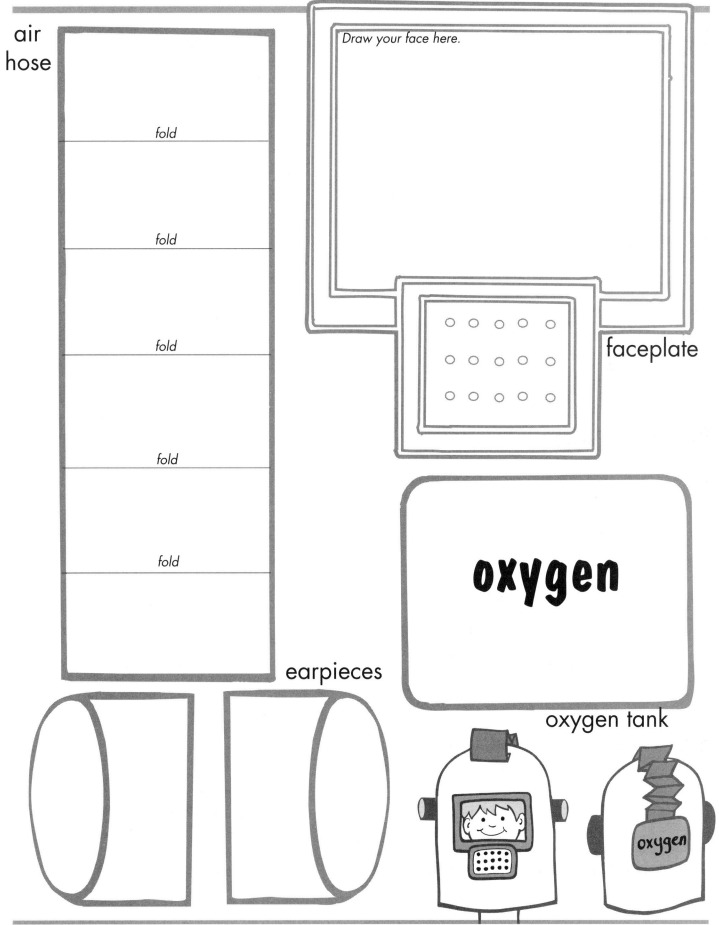

Alien

Paper Mitt Puppet

Materials

- 9" x 12" (23 x 30.5 cm) orange construction paper
- patterns on page 69
- marking pens or crayons
- scissors
- glue

Steps to Follow

1. Use the construction paper to make the basic mitt puppet.

Fold in half.

Round the top.

Open the paper and apply glue as shown.

Refold the paper and press firmly.

2. Color and cut out the pattern pieces.

3. Glue the patterns on the mitt.

4. Add details with crayons or marking pens.

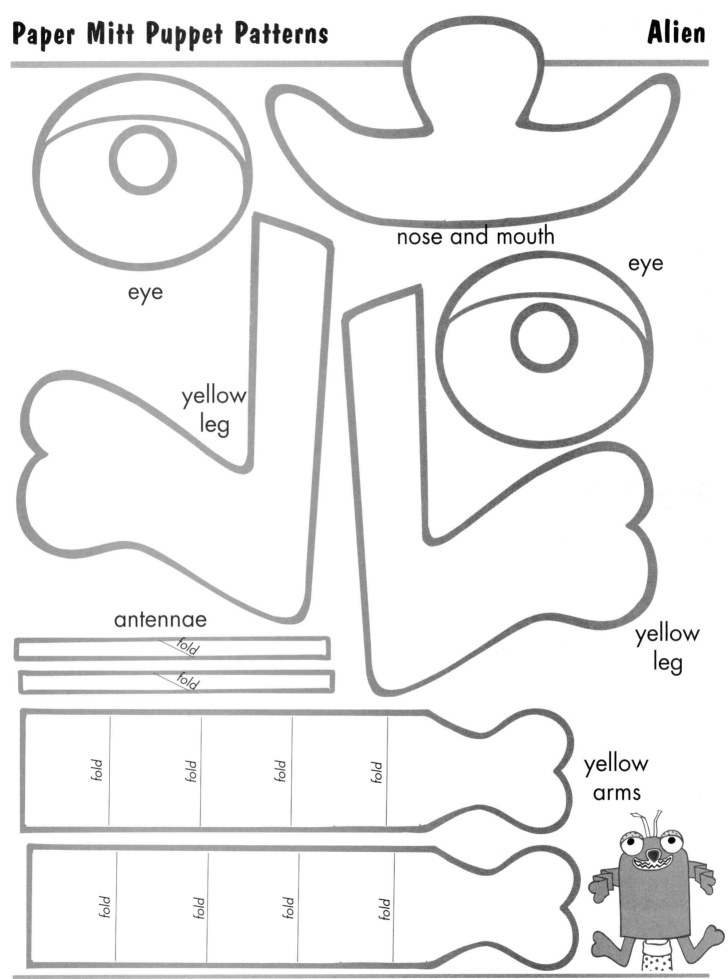

eye

nose and mouth

eye

yellow leg

yellow leg

antennae

fold

fold

yellow arms

fold *fold* *fold* *fold*

fold *fold* *fold* *fold*

Knight

Paper Mitt Puppet

Materials

- 9" x 12" (23 x 30.5 cm) gray construction paper
- patterns on page 71
- marking pens or crayons
- hole punch
- scissors
- glue

Steps to Follow

1. Use the construction paper to make the basic mitt puppet.

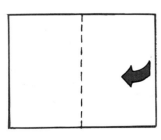

Fold in half.   *Round the top.*   *Open the paper and apply glue as shown.*   *Refold the paper and press firmly.*

2. Color and cut out the pattern pieces.

3. Glue the patterns on the mitt.

4. Punch holes along the lower edge.

faceplate

plume for helmet

Princess
Paper Mitt Puppet

Materials

- 9" x 12" (23 x 30.5 cm) tan construction paper
- patterns on page 73
- strip of lace (optional)
- marking pens or crayons
- scissors
- glue

Steps to Follow

1. Use the construction paper to make the basic mitt puppet.

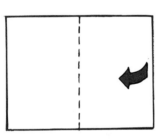

Fold in half.   *Round the top.*   *Open the paper and apply glue as shown.*   *Refold the paper and press firmly.*

2. Color and cut out the pattern pieces.

3. Glue the patterns on the mitt.

4. Add eyes, a nose, and mouth and other details with crayons or marking pens.

   Optional: Glue on a strip of lace as shown.

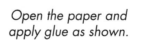

Paper Mitt Puppet Patterns

pink cheeks

hair

gold crown

Robot

Paper Mitt Puppet

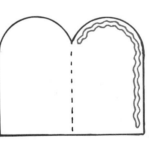

Materials

- 9" x 12" (23 x 30.5 cm) yellow construction paper
- patterns on page 75
- marking pens or crayons
- scissors
- glue

Steps to Follow

1. Use the construction paper to make the basic mitt puppet.

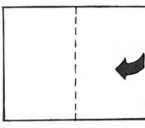

Fold in half.   *Round the top.*   *Open the paper and apply glue as shown.*   *Refold the paper and press firmly.*

2. Color and cut out the pattern pieces.

3. Glue the patterns on the mitt.

4. Add details with crayons or marking pens.

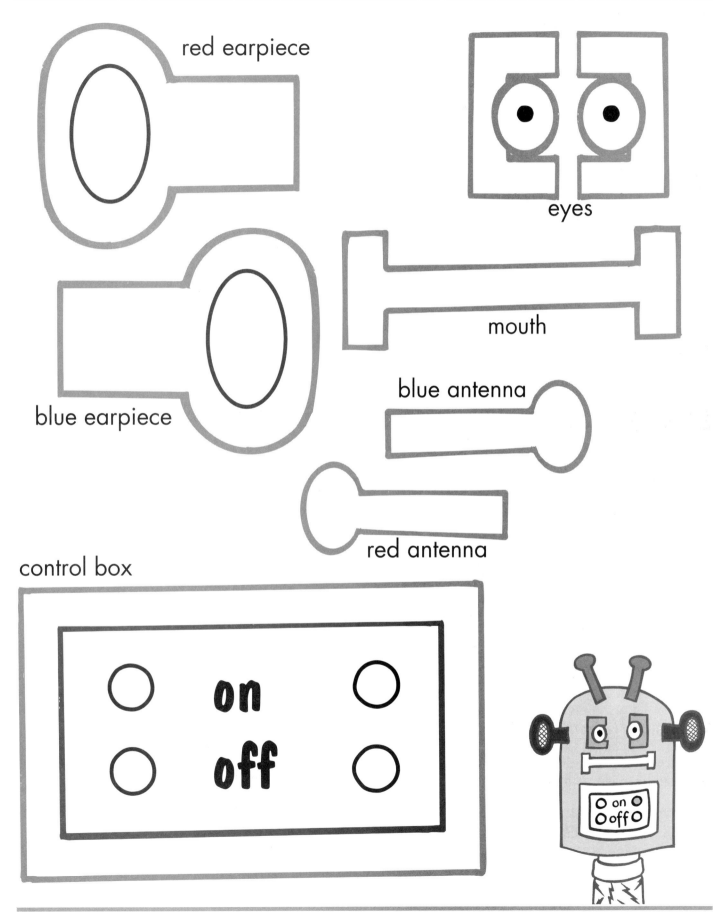

red earpiece

eyes

blue earpiece

mouth

blue antenna

red antenna

control box

on

ABC Finger Puppets

Early learners will love these easy-to-assemble puppets. Color and cut out each puppet. Glue the two pieces together along the edges, leaving the bottom open. Slip a finger inside and it's ready to use.

Aa

alligator

Bb

bear

Cc

cat

How to Make Puppets with Children • EMC 762

Dd

dog

Ee

elephant

Ff

fox

Gg

goat

Hh

hippo

Ii

iguana

How to Make Puppets with Children • EMC 762

Jj

jackrabbit

Kk

koala

Ll

lion

Mm

monkey

Nn

newt

Oo

octopus

How to Make Puppets with Children • EMC 762

Pp

pig

Qq

quail

Rr

rooster

Ss

spider

Tt

toad

Uu

unicorn

Vv

vulture

Ww

walrus

Xx

fox

Yy

yak

Zz

zebra

 How to Make Puppets with Children • EMC 762